On Conscious Love

a poetic journey

Anto Boghokian

Streaming Hope Press
Los Angeles

ISBN-13: 978-1-7331372-1-8

To all those who have the tenacity to venture on
love's journey wholeheartedly,
with resilient courage,
and a touch of humor.

CONTENTS

Heart Knocks Life

Nobody ever told me this was going to hurt,
I was not informed it lacked an off button.

I plugged in my heart, walked away and forgot
Overheated burning in passion
Started so fast, and game over so sudden
Completely I lost traction.

Got a shot through the heart when distracted by a look
but I probably will refuse to learn from this
enough times to write a poetry book.

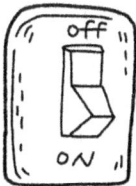

THE WILTING WILLOW

The wilting willow

lacking hope

needing sunshine and

a water drop.

Which evaporated from the pavement

The need became the ailment

wilting the willow away.

HELLO

You shot me a smile that arrested all of my attention
But right now I'm playing it cool,
and maybe we morph into fools
Standing front and center with a crowd behind and
on each side of us a whole crew
And they'll give speeches to say they always knew.
so I move forward with optimistic caution
and make sure to lay an unshakable foundation
But first I must cross the ten feet between us and start this
conversation.
"Hello...."

GONE FISHING

Hook the bait
catch the fish
clean & cook
do I like this dish?

Easy to start,
with a roulette finish.
Curious anguish
can lead up trails of beauty divine
or down ugly roads with
time to wonder what happened or
what could have been mine?
Hook the fish by the bait,
a new picture, an old portrait.
Curiosity starts to guesstimate
is this love or just a mate?
to what forecast can I relate?
Will the journey be a storm that
leads to paradise?
Will I need more than what I have, or
will less suffice?
Each situation is unique, so don't seek free advice...
   Chance to dance... and you might, just might, live out
a true tale of romance.

At the Blue-monkey

Inspired, I run with these thoughts in a space
Lacking what it takes to put action to time and place.
Wondering if our paths may cross again, and if they do,
will it be like fresh air, or an ignorant hurtful grin?
Momentary encounters can lead to a life of pondering;
what if you had let go of your soul mate and now
you're in a desert wandering
wondering
what would have been?

Screens

Hey pretty girl, where is your light?
Why is it hiding out of sight?
Your heart is heavy; your smile is slight,
enthusiasms evaporated into the night?

I can make out your picture but
can't see clearly past the screens.
Longing for a fresh start, but
what about your past re-entering the scene?

I wonder, when do diverging lives begin to fall apart?
I wonder if similar cases happen again and again—
Is it possible to reconstruct or will I collapse into sin?
But I guess it's silly to steal time with all this wondering, when
stuck at hello on this pontoon bridge pondering.

Dating As It May Seem

I collect,
pick up the pieces
in & out quicker than the breeze is
moving through,
don't stop to think
continuously on the brink
of destruction...
Inebriated conduction of life,
my collection of hearts.

POLAROID

I keep watch on your every move

whether you splash around or on the waves you groove.

I wonder about the story behind your face...

To what drumbeat do you set your life's pace?

Three seconds of contact: Hello, a snap, goodbye,

I'm just another captured memory on your iPhoto page.

Maybe one day you'll be scrolling & reminisce,

and I...

I will spend the rest of the summer trying to forget

your ocean blue eyes, charming smile, and pretty face.

TYPECAST

Love and sacrifice are useful devices
To peel your heart apart and be molded
by another's thoughts
Softened by a kiss and tangled in woven lace
I conformed without a fight.

But time proved I could
no longer bear this mold, would
no longer pay this price

Put the past away, roll the dice another day
take these lessons to the next audition
for the leading role in love's next play
and land another part you didn't audition for.

Magic Trick

A dove? An arrow? A spark?
Felt it on a bench sitting in Central Park.
Created by God, perverted by man,
the peace it's meant to give is converted to pain.
Emphasizing confusion and happy despair—
to have true love, what must one bear?

Some things don't make sense and I doubt I'll ever grasp.
Is love the heart's magic trick or is it the heart's
unbearable task?

LOVE LINES

From my rearview mirror I try to project
    what the future can bring.
Of course, I get stuck in daily traffic
    and can no longer think.
If it works out, great! But if not...what then?
How will we deal with life's curves?
Are we flexible enough to bend?

Will you puncture me with criticism
    and deflate my dreams?
Will I pressure you with expectations
    that flatten your hopes?
If either of us does, will our eyes still shine?
If we dare to face our tight-clasped hands
    and promise not to pretend,
    our love will be refined by fire
    and for a lifetime won't relent.

SHOULD'VE CHECKED TWICE

You showed up at my door
I let you in.
I held your hand but left my heart on my sleeve
dazzled by this diamond too precious to be cut.
Completely forgot to check your baggage at the door
your cancerous sin that ate you away,
   consumed you in a second
and left me to lay bleeding
   wounded
    suturing my own heart.

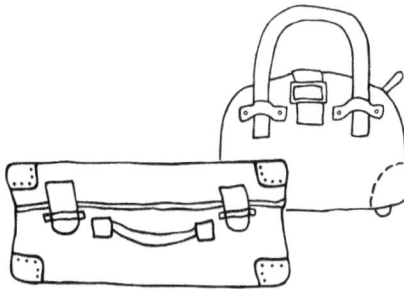

MACK TRUCK

These are my confessions, absurd, maybe, but true.

Like saloon doors I swung my heart wide open

what snuck in was you.

Smooth as ice, a heart of fire

sweetly pampered, beckoned my desire.

So I held back the flowers, but always opened the door,

At the end of each day, I just wanted one more.

Time and distance made me grow fonder of your
pretty smiling face,

You moved from one continent to the next,
and I longed for your sweet scent and embrace.

More days apart on the calendar were dated.

Holding hands slipped to fingertips,

and whatever was left...

faded.

What an unfortunate circumstance, timing or luck

I thought I was gazing into your approaching starry eyes

turns out it was really a Mack truck.

Not So Much

Jingle jangle
Sins untangle
as future plans
& underpants
slip into the air.
Wanting to but find
hard to care about
what consequences ahead.
Unfavorable when
playing Russian roulette
with an opponent
that's already dead.

Love & Pain

What now?
Where do I start?
How do I begin again?
Last night was hard.
My heart was in anguish, in pain.

Love is odd, for it reassembles your broken heart.
Exciting at first, as you fail to remember the worst.
All is good and well, the future no one can tell.

Then one day,
one hears a warning bell.
You wake up and, to your surprise, you are bleeding again.
Oh why does love have to come at the price of pain?

THE GOLD DIGGER & THE PAUPER

Our eyes meet
As we both suppress the spark,
and in the dark I realize
you're not my type.

We pretend for each other we're there. Your agenda's to find
someone with a Benz, money, and flare.
I'll make mine to take off
your underwear.

The truth hurts?
What else do you expect?
You checked in your heart for status and glamor
and shiny things;
all the diamonds and pearls won't hide the trail
of broken hearts and dirty flings.

So now you're here?
You want a quick thing?
Are you at the end of your rope?
Just looking for a ring?

C'mon baby, you give pretty girls a bad name—
stop pretendin' your shit don't stink.

GETTING OUT

Room's too small
but she wants to share.
She gets it all, I can have the bathroom stall,
she thinks it's great that we're together after all...

Misery anchors me in our golden cage
Comfortably confined but my soul apnic
How did my vision fade?
In a state of rage.

FINALLY, enough is said, the limit hit,
and I say
I'm OUT
I'm gone

I'm being true, not trying to be tough
I have to get off this boat
I'll take my chances and swim the sharky water to shore.
Yes, I might drown, or get eaten
but that's much less painful than
being forever
ignored.

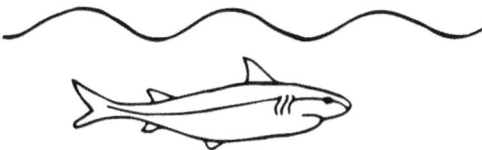

Un-Frustrated

The door has closed.
The ship has sailed.
Too little too late,
your words are meaningless,
my heart is now healed.
Begone, woman,
I'm enjoying being freed.

Movement of Years

All the years line up, then
Life throws in a fork.
Found a companion to share the wine,
but can't pop open a cork.
Life was so much simpler when I believed
babies were dropped off by a stork.
When my troubles were taken away by
a cold bottle of coke.
When I made and laughed at
my own corny joke.

ORGANIC SUGAR

My eyes came across
the intricate lace of
straight dark hair
eyes, smile, and face.

Time was racing,
my heart raced faster
but neither to doom
nor to disaster.

At the conclusion of our evening
it was no longer night
in my deepest of hearts
I felt less wrong, more right

Your picture imprinted in the depths of my heart,
smitten by your scent, I never wanted to part.
Music paced our feet,
we never skipped a beat,
and I wondered if there would be a chance
for another sugar dance.

NORTHWESTERN CHARM

We slip into the cold
degrees fall to thirty-five as
dawn transforms to dusk I dare
to ask for a dance, a chance,
to hold you tight.
Arm in arm, sweet kisses,
no one around
I surrender to tranquility...
Priceless moments never to be sold,
in your eyes I see your heart of gold.
A smile that could heal the world & bring about peace,
the most difficult of circumstances brought to ease.

Oh, 2000 miles, I wish it were two
In my heart is a space that is blessed by you.

WHEN THEN

When sorry turns back
without finding a home.
Words lack,
peace hides,
eyes gaze,
restless
One minute... an eternity.

When all my intentions are rejected
the wait for an accepted apology
is a thorn.
Maybe forgiving leaves you powerless
so you'd rather hold a grudge
and keep jabbing to stay in control.

LOVE'S RACE

I've searched for romance,
a tale that would be re-told,
like Romeo & Juliet only
together they'd grow old.

I've left no rock unturned,
spared not any gold,
for love...anything,
not much I haven't sold.

At times I've settled for counterfeit,
it wasn't quite right,
a momentary fix
until the calluses became scars.

It left me with the sour-milk
look on my face. Maybe next time
I'll be wiser,
and listen to the cautions
of Amazing Grace.

STARS AT AVENUE 23

Time flying by
Communion deepening
I want the clock to die.
To hear your sweet voice
like a waterfall as we dance
I hold you in my arms
hoping for a song
that lacks an ending.
The courtyard, the park,
surrounded by the tall city;
at dinner with you,
Avenue 23 never looked so pretty...

TANDEM

Tandem life,
What about when strife overtakes us both?
Tandem life,
When people ask if you have a husband?
I'll say I got a wife.
Tandem life
Trust is the cement.
Tandem life,
No room for just one
Will you be happy with me? Despite me?
I don't do well in pre-cut molds.
Tandem life
seems frightening so why
is everyone in a race for a tux to rent or
a white dress to buy?
Befriend wisdom: the rest of your life
is a very long time.

As My Heart Prepares

If you were a jaguar,
I'd be your prey,
just to see you approach
in that sexy sort of way.

If you were a flower petal,
or even a leaf
I'd be the morning dew,
slipping down your body daily,
to satisfy your deepest root.

If you were a waterfall,
I'd be a solid rock
you can pour over all day,
my heart would catch every single drop.
I hope they would be tears of joy &
I'd never give you cause to doubt
my faithfulness, my love.

If you were a sunset,
I'd be a camera lens,
lost in the light of your eyes
as your shining heart beams through,
causing me to amend,
to obliterate my selfish ways.

I stare at you and wonder
how such details were worked out?
Your eyes,
....your lips...
......your smile and hips...
the sound of your laughter out loud.
Blind to happiness without you by my side,
I'd never give you cause to doubt
my faithfulness, my love.

When it's just us two,
I wonder:
how can people question
the existence of God, when
there is an Angel like you?

THE GIFT

The reason for this life hits you
on just an ordinary day
beckons you to stop hiding, it can lure you out to play.
But careful, as good intentions make bad pavement
in the wrong hands it will lead you astray.

It has the power to set free, or the power to possess,
it can drive you mad or give you complete rest.
Though it feels warm, it could turn cold again,
and if you turn your back you might get stabbed, my friend.

See, the intent wasn't evil, but man made it to be
Satan's persuading power and that darn apple tree.

This answer I found simple & amazing
comes from heaven above...
It's selfless, patient, and caring,
the creator calls it love.

ABOUT THE AUTHOR

Anto Boghokian is an Armenian-American actor, poet, and producer residing in Los Angeles, California. Born and raised in Kuwait, he spent the summers in the countryside of Lebanon. While visiting his grandparents in the United States in 1990, the events of the Gulf War suddenly made Glendale, California his new home. For twenty-one years he struggled to gain permanent residency as an immigrant and used writing (particularly poetry) as an emotional and creative outlet. He admits, "The only place I could be completely honest was my poems."

His first book, *1000 Hours*, gained enough traction that an accompanying *1000 Hours Journal* was published.

In *On Conscious Love: a poetic journey*, Anto shares from experiences of love at first glance, thoughts on lost chance, and the daily dance into and out of the stories that transform the texture of our lives.

If you would like to book Anto for a spoken-word performance, a book signing, or workshops, please contact Anto through his personal website, AntoBoghokian.com.

www.ingramcontent.com/pod-product-compliance
Lightning Source LLC
Chambersburg PA
CBHW070458050426
42449CB00012B/3031